SPIRIT ANIMAL

COLORING BOOK

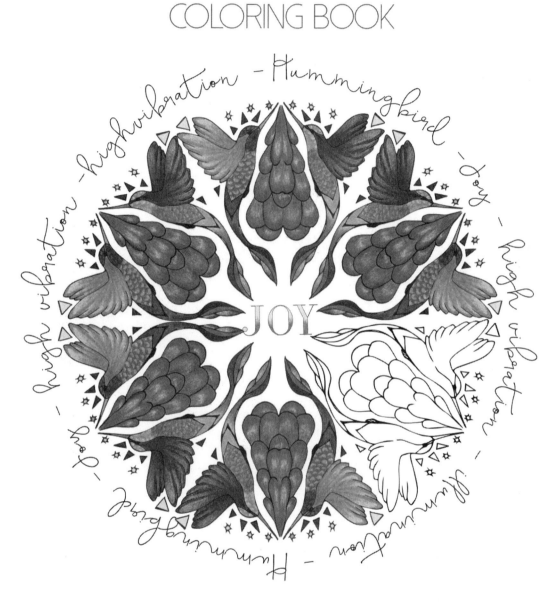

SARAH WILDER

HAY HOUSE

Carlsbad, California • New York • London • Sydney
Johannesburg • Vancouver • New Delhi

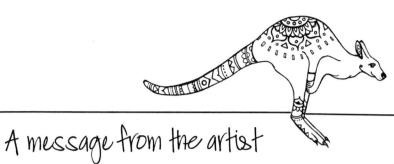

A message from the artist

Working with animal magic has been something I have intuitively done since I was a little girl. Looking back at my childhood photographs, you rarely see me without a dog, cat, chicken, or some form of wildlife.

As a young adult, I followed two very different careers: fashion design and animal husbandry. My ego called me to fashion, but my soul called me to work with animals. I spent my time balancing both for many years, yo-yoing from studying clothing production to native animal rehabilitation. On weekends, I would spend one day sewing and designing, the next volunteering at the Australia Zoo wildlife hospital. After a while, I ended up finding more financial success and opportunity in fashion, so I chose to put the animal career goals on hold.

I still feel a deep connection to animals; they make me happy and peaceful. I'm instinctively drawn to them and I have such a profound respect for them and their gifts. The term for my passion and intuitive connection to animals is "Zoomancy." This is the art of divination or intuitive insight, based on the observation of animals. I believe that everyone has the ability to be a Zoomancer. It is something we don't have to learn; it is within us all, if we are so inclined.

This book is my opportunity to show animals my gratitude and hopefully inspire others to do a bit of inner work and reconnect with the non-human spirits that share this earth with us. This is our chance to visit the places where our instincts and intuitive voices lie, using stunning imagery and familiar animal figures to guide us.

Introduction to mandalas

Pronounced *MUN-DAH-LAH*, this beautiful form of self-expression originates from a Sanskrit word meaning "circle" or "center." Mandalas are embraced by many cultures, who use different methods to interpret this art form (sand, medicine wheels, architecture, and art). However, the essence and meaning is always the same, with mandalas representing wholeness, unity, healing, and harmony.

Mandalas are not just another form of art. They are used in conjunction with healing, meditation, reflection, relaxation, balance, reconnection, and mindfulness, and also as a form of medicine.

As circles and spirals make up so much of our own environment, it is no wonder we feel a connection to mandalas. The sun, moon, and planets are all circular, and we refer to our friends, family, and community as "circles"—all equal, all one, with no beginning or end. We have a subconscious love for mandalas because we are genetically, scientifically, and spiritually connected to them. Now we are starting to connect with them consciously too.

Choosing an image

Just select an animal you feel connected to on a particular day, or make a selection based on a word you want to bring attention to in your life. Flip through the pages until you feel called by a particular animal, or head to the list on the next page and select a word you wish to focus on.

Choosing colors

There are two approaches you can take to choosing the colors for your creative meditation mandalas:

Intuitive selection—an organic approach that honors your inner flow, starting the coloring process with little thought or planning. This is ideal for anyone wanting to uncover some subconscious feelings through color therapy. After completing your artwork, you are encouraged to meditate on the colors and design (perhaps refer to a color meaning chart) to uncover some of the inner feelings that may have surfaced during your meditation.

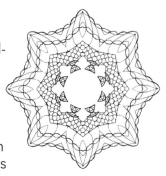

Intentional selection—use this approach when you are seeking a specific outcome, whether it be to promote healing, unlock your creativity, or inject some motivation and passion into your life.

Tips for coloring

- Contrast is important—color extremes add drama and complement one another!
- Keep some white space to help bring the detail and colors out in your design.
- Start from the inside out to prevent smudging your work and to help you to see which color to use next.
- A well-lit, quiet space free of clutter is recommended.
- Meditation music (or a peaceful soundtrack) helps to avoid distraction.

A
Abundance: Pig, 67; Rabbit, 69; Turkey, 85
Action: Lionfish, 50
Adaptation / Adaptability / Adaptable: Clownfish, 16; Fox, 34; Pig, 67
Advantage: Giraffe, 37
Adventure: Komodo Dragon, 48
Angels: Bluebird, 7
Authenticity: Parrotfish, 62
Awareness: Moth, 58

B
Balance: Kangaroo, 44; Magpie, 55; Zebra, 91
Beauty: Lady Beetle, 49
Bravery: Koi, 47

C
Celebration: Camel, 10; Parrotfish, 62
Change: Butterfly, 9
Cleanse: Frog, 35
Clever: Fox, 34
Commitment: Bee, 5
Communication: Toucan, 84
Community: Ant, 2; Flamingo, 33
Compassion: Elephant, 31
Confidence: Bear, 4; Lion, 51; Toucan, 84
Connection: Elephant, 31; Hawk, 38; Kangaroo, 44; Wolf, 89

Contentment: Iguana, 41; Tortoise, 83
Co-operation: Dolphin, 25
Courage: Parrotfish, 62; Tiger, 82
Creation / Creativity / Creative Expression: Bowerbird, 8; Cockatoo, 17; Orangutan, 60; Spider, 77
Curiosity: Alpaca, 1
Cycles: Cicada, 15; Crab, 20

D
Defensive: Magpie, 55
Depth: Whale Shark, 88
Desire: Eel, 30
Discernment: Moose, 57
Divinity: Cat, 12; Unicorn, 87
Dreams / Dream Weaver: Bat, 3; Spider, 77
Drive: Eel, 30; Horse, 39

E
Emotional Strength: Lionfish, 50
Enchantment: Butterfly, 9
Endurance: Camel, 10
Energy: Chameleon, 14
Evolution: Snail, 75

F
Family: Gouldian Finch, 32; Macaw, 54
Femininity: Cow, 18
Flow: Jellyfish, 43
Focus: Hawk, 38; Rooster, 70

Freedom: Cockatoo, 17; Horse, 39
Friendship: Gouldian Finch, 32; Flamingo, 33

G
Gateway: Crow, 23
Gifts: Lionfish, 50
Goals: Komodo Dragon, 48
Good Luck / Luck: Bee, 5; Cricket, 21; Lady Beetle, 49
Grace: Deer, 24
Gratefulness: Turkey, 85
Growth: Caterpillar, 13
Guidance: Hawk, 38

H
Happiness: Bluebird, 7
Harmony: Swan, 81; Zebra, 91
Healing: Frog, 35
Home: Macaw, 54
Honesty: Rooster, 70
Honor: Turkey, 85

I
Illumination: Hummingbird, 40
Imagination: Dragonfly, 27
Impulse: Eel, 30
Individualism: Mandarin Fish, 56; Wolf, 89
Influence: Chameleon, 14; Toucan, 84

BOWER
BIRD

selflessness

creativity

romance

BUTTER
FLY

CAMEL

celebration

endurance

innovation

10

CATERPILLAR

CHAMELEON

Observation – Energy – Influence – Observation – Energy – Influence – Observation – Energy – Influence – Observation

CICADA

Divine Timing – Cycles – Vibration – Divine Timing – Cycles – Vibration – Divine Timing – Cycles – Vibration – Divine Timing – Cycles – Vibration –

CLOWNFISH

Teamwork

Adaptation

Respect

COCKATOO

freedom

travel

creative expression

Wander

Trickster

Shapeshift

COYOTE

CRAB

cycles

trust

safety

CROCODILE

Primal Force

Patience

Wisdom

CROW

Messenger — Gateway — Magick — Messenger — Gateway — Magick — Messenger — Gateway — Magick — Messenger — Gateway — Magick

Sensitivities — Grace — Retreat — Sensitivities — Grace — Retreat — Sensitivities — Grace — Retreat — Sensitivities — Grace — Retreat —

DEER

DOLPHIN

Co-operation – Peace – Play – Co-operation – Peace – Play – Co-operation – Peace – Play – Co-operation – Peace – Play –

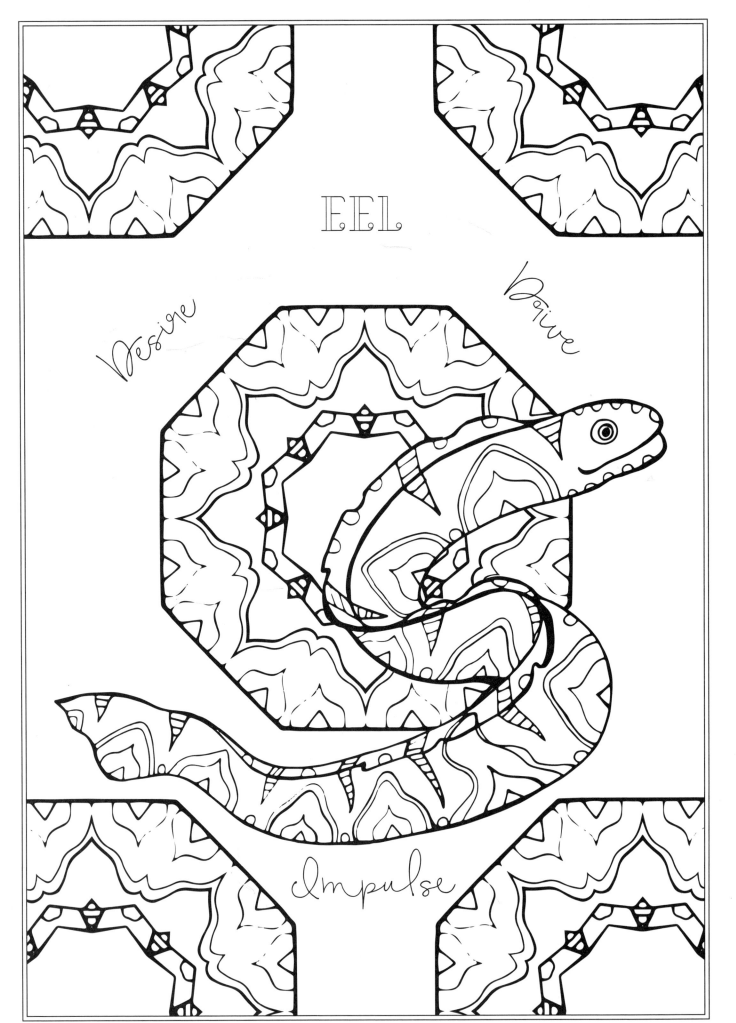

EEL

Desire

Naive

Impulse

30

FLAMINGO

Friendship - Community - Tradition - Friendship - Community - Tradition - Friendship - Community - Tradition - Friendship - Community - Tradition

FOX

GECKO

Sensitivity – Sensuality – Sacrifice – Sensuality – Sacrifice – Sensitivity – Sensuality – Sacrifice – Sensitivity

GIRAFFE

Understanding – Advantage – Perception – Understanding – Advantage – Perception – Understanding – Advantage – Perception – Understanding – Advantage – Perception –

HAWK

Connection

Focus

Guidance

Motivation - Freedom - Drive - Motivation - Freedom - Drive - Motivation - Freedom - Drive - Motivation - Freedom - Drive

HORSE

illumination – Hummingbird – Joy – high vibration – high vibration – illumination – Hummingbird – Joy

JOY

IGUANA

Simplicity

Contentment

Observe

JAGUAR

Intention

Solitary

Power

Surrender

Flow

Source

JELLYFISH

Stamina

Connection

KANGAROO

Balance

Bravery

Perseverance

KOI

Success

KOMODO DRAGON

Adventure

Goals

Warrior

LADY
BEETLE

Luck - Beauty - Inquisitive - Luck - Beauty - Inquisitive - Luck - Beauty - Inquisitive - Luck - Beauty

LION FISH

Action

Gifts

Emotional Strength

LION

Confidence - Pride - Power - Confidence - Pride - Power - Confidence - Pride - Power - Confidence - Pride - Power -

FRILLED
NECK
LIZARD

Timing

Pride

Presentation

MACAW

Family

Home

True Colors

MAGPIE

Defensive

Balance

Story-Teller

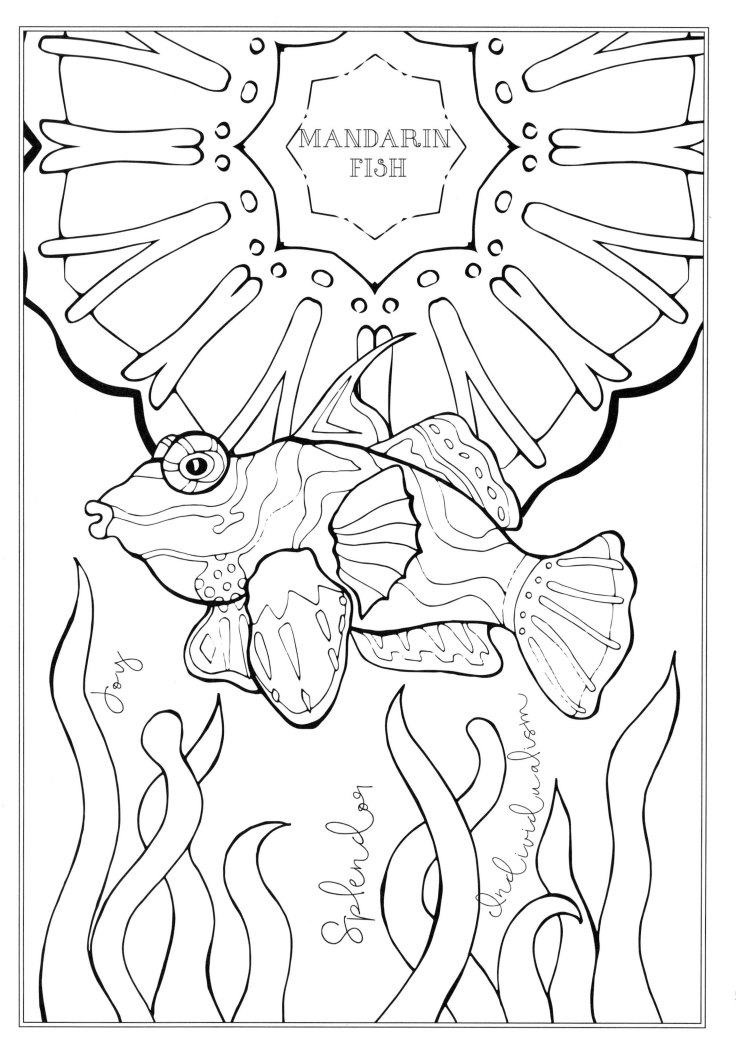

MANDARIN
FISH

Joy

Splendor

Individualism

MOOSE

Respect

Mindfulness

Discernment

MOTH

Knowing

Awareness

Vulnerability

OCTOPUS

Intelligence

Mystery   Resourceful

59

ORANGUTAN

Play

Creation

Inner Child

OWL

Intuition - Insight - Intuition - Wisdom - Insight - Wisdom - Insight - Strength - Wisdom - Intuition - Wisdom

PEACOCK

Inspiration – Passion – Insight – Inspiration – Passion – Insight – Inspiration – Passion – Insight – Inspiration

Self-discipline

Purpose

Renewal

PENGUIN

64

PHOENIX

Power — Rise — Renewal — Power — Rise — Renewal — Power — Rise — Renewal — Power — Rise — Renewal —

PIG

Opportunity

Abundance

Adaptability

PRAYING
MANTIS

Patience — Stillness — Persistence — Patience — Stillness — Persistence — Patience — Stillness — Persistence

RABBIT

Sensitive – Abundance – Procreation – Sensitive – Abundance – Procreation – Sensitive – Abundance – Procreation

ROOSTER

Focus

Honesty

Time-Keeper

SCORPION

Résilience — Passion — Solitude — Résilience — Passion — Solitude — Passion — Solitude — Résilience — Passion — Solitude — Résilience

SEA
HORSE

Patience — Love — Vulnerability — Patience — Love — Vulnerability — Patience — Love — Vulnerability — Patience — Love — Vulnerability

SHARK

SLOTH

Wisdom

Peace

Priority

SNAIL

Evolution

Progress

Self-Reliance

SNAKE

Transformation - Shedding - Life Force - Transformation - Shedding - Life Force - Transformation - Shedding - Life Force - Transformation - Shedding - Life Force

SPIDER

Creativity

Dreamweaver

Teacher

SQUIRREL

Plan

Playfulness

Problem
Solve

Sensitivity

Stillness

Regeneration

STARFISH

STORK

Motherhood

Prosperity

Renewal

SWAN

Purity – Harmony – Mirror – Purity – Harmony – Mirror – Harmony – Mirror – Purity – Harmony – Mirror – Purity

Contentment

Treasure

TORTOISE

Longevity

Communication – Influence – Confidence – Communication – Influence – Confidence – Communication – Influence – Confidence –

TOUCAN

TURKEY

Honor

Abundance

Gratefulness

Depth

Reservation

Presence

WHALE SHARK

WOLF

Connection - Loyalty - Individualism - Connection - Loyalty - Individualism - Connection - Loyalty - Individualism - Connection - Loyalty - Individualism

WOOD
PECKER

Network — Opportunity — Resourcefulness — Network — Opportunity — Resourcefulness — Opportunity — Resourcefulness — Network

ZEBRA

Balance

Harmony

Peace

Published and distributed in the United States by: Hay House, Inc.: www.hayhouse.com® • ***Published and distributed in Australia by:*** Hay House Australia Pty. Ltd.: www.hayhouse.com.au • ***Published and distributed in the United Kingdom by:*** Hay House UK, Ltd.: www.hayhouse.co.uk • ***Published and distributed in the Republic of South Africa by:*** Hay House SA (Pty), Ltd.: www.hayhouse.co.za • ***Distributed in Canada by:*** Raincoast Books: www.raincoast.com • ***Published in India by:*** Hay House Publishers India: www.hayhouse.co.in

Cover and interior design: Sarah Wilder
Cover and interior illustrations: Nicole Brown, Niche Creative

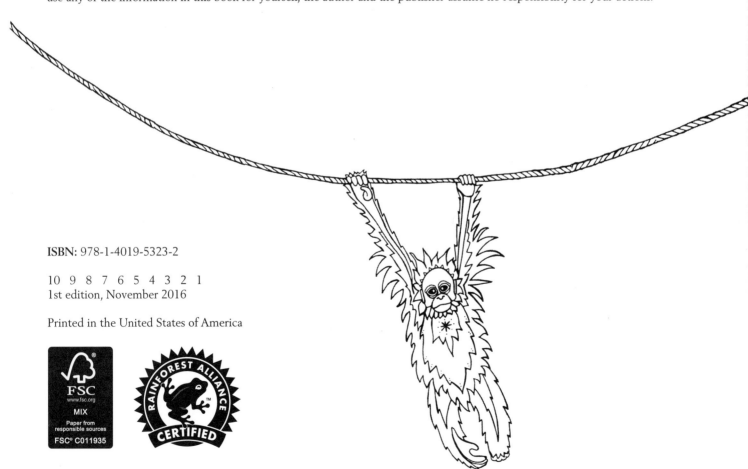

ISBN: 978-1-4019-5323-2

10 9 8 7 6 5 4 3 2 1
1st edition, November 2016

Printed in the United States of America